Not Proven: Fair Game

A H FitzSimons

Copyright © 2023 by A H FitzSimons

The right of A H FitzSimons to be identified as the author of this work has been asserted by him in accordance with the Copyright, Designs and Patents Act 1988

All rights reserved. No part of this publication may be reproduced, stored in a retrieval system, or transmitted in any other form or by any means, electronic, mechanical, photocopying, recording or otherwise without the prior written permission of the copyright holder

Published by Open Path Books 2023 ISBN 978-1-8383829-4-0

Inspired by the screenplay *Silent Cries* by Monika Richardson and Jimmy Pace

Not Proven: Fair Game is the sequel to the novel *HK9*
ISBN 978-1-8383829-3-3

The characters in this publication are fictitious and any resemblance to real persons, living or dead, is purely coincidental

For Julie

Acknowledgements

My thanks to Rubén Manso (editing) and Ozzy Eyre (cover design).

The 'not proven' verdict is exclusive to Scots law, where in addition to the verdicts of 'guilty' and 'not guilty', a verdict of 'not proven' can be given. It is widely accepted that this verdict indicates a belief that the accused is guilty but there is insufficient evidence to secure a conviction. There have been several attempts to abolish this verdict, most recently by an SNP led Scottish Government. However, at time of publication (June 2023) the 'not proven' verdict remains in use in Scotland.

Not Proven: Fair Game

PROLOGUE

At first he thinks he's waking from a dream. Then he feels cold. He feels the wind against him; he feels movement, rolling, rising up, sinking down.

His eyes remain closed, but his other senses begin to relay more data. He can hear crashing. Something light is hitting his legs and face. He wonders if he is dreaming of when he was a child. But he knows this isn't a dream. So why is he unable to move? Why does he feel something is terribly wrong? He has to think, to work this out.

Drugs. But he's never taken drugs. Then he must have been drugged. That's why he's thinking so slowly: that's why his body isn't moving. But what drug? He knows this field; he studied it for months until he knew it backwards. He knows what drugs to use to make people sleep, to neutralize someone's will, to make them compliant, to allow him to take total control. He knows the right amounts for everyone, and the many influencing factors. So what drug had been used on him? How much of it, and how long has it been in his system? Why, though? And where is he?

That doesn't matter now: all that matters is adrenaline, getting it in to his system to flush out the drug. He orders himself to think of something that makes him angry ... or afraid. This isn't a dream, he reminds himself, so open your eyes!

He's hit again, this time his face and body. It must be water, he can feel it running down his face, across his lips. He licks them and tastes salt. Sea water ... OPEN YOUR EYES!

Suddenly he's blinking, focusing; but his mind can't handle the immensity of what's there. Two blues face him:

dark, massive, monstrous waves, and above them a light sky, but it's the waves that hold him. They terrify him.

Now he hears more than the crashing of the waves, more than the howling wind. He hears voices. He sees two people in oilskins ten feet away, talking. He tries to call out but his lips won't move. He pulls forwards and feels his wrists now – burning, rubbing, but against what?

Rope. He is tied up. Why? He has been taken from somewhere, but where? What was his last memory?

No, that doesn't matter. Adrenaline is all that matters now, flush the drug out of your system. Adrenaline will save you.

What are they doing? Look at those waves, look at that sea. It looks so different now, so beautiful and so—

No, don't think that.

I have to, I need the adrenaline.

The sea is solitude: the loneliest, darkest death. A death that no one will share, no one will ever know about, out here, in the vastness of the dark blue ... in oblivion.

Voices approaching – what is the accent? With the wind he can barely make out what's being said. Someone behind him, loosening the bindings. Isn't that good? But he's feeling more adrenaline. His wrists are now held by their hands. His feet drag along the deck as they lead him. His body is flooding with adrenaline but he is as limp as a rag doll. He can do nothing to stop this. They are talking to each other, ignoring him completely. It's as if he doesn't exist. Perhaps he doesn't. Perhaps he never did.

He is dragged towards the main deck area, then they are at the side of the ship. He is being lifted on to the rails, and all he can look at is the dark blue waves; they are spellbinding. Can his life be so insignificant now? What happened?

As he is tilted forward, he remembers something – someone walking up to him, then a jarring sensation, and his legs buckling, his world spinning.

He tears his eyes away from the dark blue and, looking at the man on his right, he sees cracked lips, a broken nose and brown eyes.

He recognizes the accent now, but it doesn't matter. Nothing matters anymore. He knows his death is in the sea, the blinding truth of his insignificance. It hadn't always been like that – he'd had a life. He was young, he had a family. Someone was taking that away from him. He didn't have to ask why. He remembered everything. He knew why.

The man lifts a block of concrete and tips it over the side. Before he hears it hit the water, his body is propelled forwards.

For a second, as he flies through the air, a wave of hope catches him – this is the point where you wake from your dreams.

The cold impact is like nothing he's ever felt before. It is life and death coming together for one final shock. All his senses are exploding. He clamps his eyes shut, as if he can shut out everything so that nothing will be real – this won't be real, it can't be real – but his mouth is opening now, the dark blue is rushing in ...

Two years earlier

'Ah, there you are. You look tired, dear. How about a cuppa?'

Arthur Anderson threw his tweed jacket over a chair and headed straight for the drinks cabinet. 'Not right now, thanks. I'm going to have a scotch, will you join me?'

Caroline walked through to the kitchen. 'Why not. Let me just pop this in the oven, and I'll be right with you.'

Mrs Anderson hurriedly wrapped foil over the top of a chicken, opened the oven door - whilst lifting her head to avoid the rush of heat - slid the tray on to the middle shelf, set the timer, and was drying her hands as she entered the living room. She knew all too well that her husband needed to talk. When he'd had a bad day at work the first thing he wanted was a drink.

She kissed him on the cheek, took the glass he handed her, and they both sat.

'Well, how did things go?' she asked.

Arthur looked at his wife, her tight grey jersey and black leggings showing off her figure. She was in her early sixties but still retained the beauty of her youth. Her husband shook his head and smiled. The day had started badly and steadily gone downhill, but all it took was one look at the woman a few feet away to level the playing field.

'I was able to speak to the survivor of Delta Five today.'

'Oh, I think you told me about him, used to be a sergeant in the SAS, one of their top marksmen. Did he not end up in hospital somewhere in Spain? But that was a while ago—wait, wasn't he the one that went to prison?'

Arthur looked down, swirling the golden liquid up against the sides of the glass before taking a long sip. 'That was a bar brawl; killed the other man – a civilian; a favourite amongst the locals, so there were several witnesses saying that the soldier started it. When he was found guilty the army disowned him: dishonourably discharged. But he got his act together, served his time, and after his release we took him on. He was our best sniper.'

'Was? I take it he's not returning then.'

'No. He's broken. He was in a pain unit in Barcelona for four months, then we had him transferred to a military hospital in Wiltshire. That was a year ago. Doesn't matter how much care you give them. Broke is broke. What do you do with a broken soldier?'

'Well, I don't suppose there's much you can do.'

'You know, I asked Hopkins the same question, and she gave me the exact same answer.' The psychologist lifted the glass to his lips, tilted his head back and downed what liquid remained. 'And that conversation is a problem.'

'Why?'

'He'd arrived early and was sitting two feet away from my office door when the conversation took place.'

'You think he heard?'

'I think ... probably. Oh, I don't know for sure. If he did, he didn't let on.'

Caroline took a sip from her glass, then cradling it between both her hands, began to rotate it one way then back, all the time waiting patiently for her husband to continue ...

'His medical report isn't good. Near constant flashbacks to when he was tortured. At night they give him hypnotics to knock him out, but when he sleeps he has nightmares – not for long though: his screams wake him. He has no appetite and that makes for a gaunt, haunted figure. He's a shadow of the man he used to be, physically and mentally.'

'So, what did you tell him?'

'What could I say—?'

Caroline smiled, 'Come on Arthur, you aways come up with something. Always. Even it's only gut instinct and there's zero research to back it up.'

'Of course, you're right, I had to tell him something. It's basic stuff, most of us will have done it at some point in our life, even though we're often not aware of it. When life becomes unbearable and we can't cope and are on the verge of despair, we often pretend we're someone else. But I asked him to go further than simple pretence, I asked him to eat, sleep and think he's this person - to become him - as far as he is able.'

'Become who?'

'That's up to him. A figure he identifies with, someone who can keep their head ... the man from Rudyard Kipling's *If—*'

'I've heard you frequently say that that poem's an ideal, a goal. I don't think there's a man alive who lives up to it.'

'The first part - the man who keeps his head, the man who stays calm no matter what is happening around him, and inside him. No matter how bad it is, this man remains in control.'

Caroline smiled, 'And that's the man I married. I knew you would come up with something. What do you think his chances are?'

'Well, he's being given the perfect opportunity to make a fresh start. On Friday he's being given a new identity of his choosing. Next week he'll be taken up to his accommodation - a cottage has been purchased for him in a quiet retirement town on the east coast of Scotland. He's from that region originally; family moved to England when he was eight. The cottage is on the sea front. He'll have a physiotherapist visiting him weekdays, and a home help will visit every day to make sure he's looking after himself.'

'That's a lot of trouble being taken over one man. Who's responsible?'

'Helen Gleason, she's in charge now.'

'Does she know him?'

Arthur shook his head. 'Gleason sent his team in to capture Robertson without backup.'

'Robertson! What—not even one team?'

'There was a time factor - a short window. It was a risk, and now Gleason's doing everything she can to make amends. Considering the way his military career ended she must have pulled a lot of strings to get him transferred to a military hospital.'

Caroline shook her head as she tried to take in this new information. 'So ... he was tortured by Robertson?'

Arthur nodded.

'For how long?'

'We don't know. He doesn't know. We think around twenty-four hours.'

Caroline let out a long sigh.

Arthur continued, 'And he was asking one hell of lot of questions about her.'

'What did you tell him?'

'The truth. With someone who's confiding in you, it always has to be the truth. The moment you lie to them they'll know, and you can forget about seeing them again. In these situations, trust and truth are inseparable - there's no such thing as a white lie.' After a long pause the psychologist continued, 'He knows everything I know about Robertson, which considering it includes everything Gleason told me, is quite a lot, though I don't know what good it will do him. Anyway, we're doing all we can. But in the end, he'll probably drink himself to death ... or walk in to the sea.'

Caroline nodded in resignation.

Arthur, recognizing the look on his wife's face, shifted to a more optimistic mode. He hadn't thought this conversation through and hadn't taken in to account his wife's compassion – that hearing about the misfortune of a man she'd never met would upset her.

'There's still a chance though, Caroline. He's a hard case. There's always a chance with that kind of man – all it takes is someone to push the right buttons.'

PART ONE

The Button

1

February

I could feel the heat, as if I was being cooked inside an oven. My mouth was bone dry and I desperately wanted a drink, but there was nothing to drink. I could feel the butt of the rifle in my shoulder; looking through the scope I watched as the paint blistered on the window frames of the cottage. Plants wilted and died; birds staggered around in small circles before falling on their sides where they lay unmoving. It was too hot to think properly; but despite that, I could feel it, and hear it. Oh, I could hear it alright. That voice was unmistakable – the voice inside me crying out the warning that something was wrong, that something terrible was about to happen. What, though?
You know what's wrong.
Robertson. She was what was wrong. She was out there, somewhere, everywhere.
She was here. She'd worked her way around, she had butchered the others ...
So why are you looking at the cottage?
You know where she is. She's here.
I twisted around, 'Cover your six!' I cried, but as I turned I saw the terrible look on my friend's face, and the dark figure step from behind him, moving towards me ... Too slow, I was always too slow. That was the moment the pain broke through. That's when I woke screaming.

It's not the dream that wakes me, it's my screams. Why did I keep dreaming the same event? Did it matter? It was only a dream. But it didn't stop when I stopped screaming. Of course there was the pain, slowly spreading to every point she'd targeted. I lay in silence, my first task was to fade out the pain, but that wasn't so simple. Time should have been passing, but it seemed to stand still, seconds stretched out. Then, finally ... her voice - soft, gentle, almost a whisper.

'Who sent you?'

I was wide awake and I could hear her. There was no other sign of her though, just the voice. Just the pain. A pain that flattened my resistance. Resistance built up over long years, snuffed out in the snap of someone's fingers. The pain that reached inside my skull, reached inside my past and tore my world apart.

Suddenly I could feel her breath on my right ear. Then the whisper, different this time, 'A name. An address. That's all I want. I'm not asking for government secrets. One name, one address.'

When I failed to respond she would take hold of one of the needles, usually from my knee, and gently twist it, one way, then another, then another ... then move to another point of my body; then work on both at the same time; then, inserting more needles. That's how it went on, for minutes, for hours, for an eternity ... a waking dream where I could see the walls of the giant room, the hooks hanging from the ceiling, old broken-down machines. In hospital they told me it was a disused abattoir. But back in Andorra, when I was in that room, working out where I was hadn't entered my mind after the pain broke through. After that, nothing seemed to matter - other than making the pain stop.

You have to get up.

Why? I don't want to get up. I want to lie here.

I had no reason to get up. I lay in bed, looking at the ceiling, and I'd go through it again and again and again. Why hadn't I followed my instincts and alerted everyone that we were walking into a trap? Why hadn't I? Why? Then I'd play out different scenarios – in each one, I had stopped the ambush from occurring. Scenarios where I killed Robertson and saved my friends. Saved myself from those needles, saved the horrors of knowing where those needles went.

Get up.

Eventually I looked across at the bedside clock. I'd been trying to change the past for the last three hours. I knew I was wasting what life I had left, yet I couldn't stop. Over 16 months had passed and I still couldn't accept that it had happened. It seemed I was firmly stuck in the past, and until I changed it, I wouldn't be able to move forwards.

But you can't change the past.

I got up, threw on some clothes, limped over to the window, and drew back the curtains. The view from my bedroom window and the front of the building was totally dominated by tall trees that stood between the cottage and the golf course. I should have kept the curtains shut. As I stood looking out at the wall of wood and leaves my mind went back to a training exercise where our squad, having set up camp on the edge of a forest, sat in a group eating our rations. Josh Barclay, one of the men I knew from Basic, came up in conversation. His twelve-year-old son had dived head first off a motorway overpass. Josh was a good guy, and this had crushed him. No one knew the reason. As the conversation began we were all asking the same questions.

'Didn't the boy think about his parents, and that they would have to ID the body?'

'Surely he would have given some thought to the others who were around at the time.'

'What about his brothers?'

'What about his Mother?'

'What about Josh?'

Then someone spoke about a tribe in Africa where the tribesmen live solely in the present tense. If they were put in prison they died, because they couldn't imagine a future when they would be released.

We mulled that over for a while, and decided that would probably be a big part of the reason. The boy must have been so immersed in the despair of the present that he couldn't see the future. If there was no future then there was no point in looking for a way out, because there was no way out. There would also be no aftermath to his death, nothing to clear up, no body to identify. Death was the only solution.

I turned away from the window and sat down on the bed. Is that where I'm at, to finish the job that Robertson had left unfinished, back in Andorra? Back in that oven? Josh's son may not have been able to see a way out of the present and, as such, was unable to see a future. It was different for me. I wasn't in the present, I was stuck in the past trying to change the mistakes I'd made. I was sick of the pain in my knees and other joints, sick of Robertson invading my world, of her whispering in my ear. I was sick of the past, yet I couldn't escape it. I tried though. I drank bourbon, I watched films and clips on YouTube. But it didn't make a difference, I was immersed in a horror version of Groundhog Day, a day where I went through the same mistakes; and no matter how much I tried and how many different scenarios I played out it was never going to make a difference. I was always going to be unable to change the events that had taken place that day. I couldn't learn from it. My friends were all dead. No matter what I did, I was going to be stuck in that day forever. I thought about the three academics who had tried to solve infinity, but only succeeded in driving themselves to insanity and suicide.

I was doing the same, in trying to change the past I was trying to do something that was impossible but, unlike them, I knew I was doing it. I knew I was driving myself to insanity, yet I remained fixed on course, intent on pressing the self-destruct button every day. I had no reason not to.

What do you do with a broken soldier? Put a bullet in his brain. Put him out of his misery.

'Breakfast is on the table.'

Emily, my carer, had a back-door key. I had been so deep in thought I hadn't heard her busying herself around the kitchen.

'Thanks, but I'm not hungry.' I called out.

'How many times are we gonna have this conversation. You need to eat.'

As I limped through to the kitchen, I glanced over at the plateful the girl had prepared.

'A fry up. Is that healthy?' I said.

'It's grilled, and you're the last person to be counting calories. You're skin and bone, you need high-calorie foods.'

I limped over to the window. Beyond the wooden framework of the open porch, there was the wide expanse of the beach and the sea beyond – light gold contrasting with dark blue. I glanced upwards at a grey sky.

So that's what you look like.

'I'm not hungry.'

Emily was not discouraged. 'You said that already. You said it yesterday, and the day before yesterday, and all last week. You need to make a start. You need to force a few mouthfuls down.'

'I don't like eating alone.'

She stared at me for a few seconds, then turned around and headed for the cupboard, she was back at the table with a bowl of muesli and a glass of milk, she poured half the glass into the bowl, then slid the glass over beside my plate. I had thought she would leave with a parting comment about how her job was to put food in front of me, it was entirely up to me whether I ate it. I was surprised when she sat down and started eating the muesli.

I liked her being around, after all she was certainly nice to look at. She had a wide face, and thick pronounced cheekbones. She reminded me of Maryanka, the Cossack girl in Tolstoy's novella. Even her irises were black, or such a dark shade of brown they were indistinguishable from her pupils. A half-inch scar ran across her right cheekbone, an imperfection that somehow added to her beauty. And she had a good build on her; although in her mid-to-late thirties she looked like she ran along the beach every morning. Yet there was this odd contradiction between her youthful athleticism and the unfathomable sadness in those jet-black eyes.

She'd taken a step to help me. Should I respond, should I eat everything on the plate and drink the half glass of milk for no other reason than a need to have some beauty in my world? Was that enough of a reason?

Evidently it was, and it turned out to be the first time since Andorra that I'd eaten a full breakfast.

I sat in front of the TV for the rest of the day, ate a couple of packets of crisps, an apple, and had a go at a bar of chocolate but I found it far too sweet. I figured my body craved protein; it made sense.

I looked over my box of meds. I'd forgotten to take my tablets this morning, but my attention was now on the Zopiclone. A pure hypnotic that knocked me out inside 15 minutes. I picked up the packet, wondering how many it would take to do the job permanently. On a really good night

I could sleep for as long as three hours before being visited by the sound of Robertson whispering in my ear. I took two of the tablets, swallowing them down with the remnants of a bottle of Wild Turkey. I studied the rest of the packet; it was tempting, just to put an end to the fear, an end to the pain. Even if I had everything back – my strength, my mobility – I'd still be a victim of Robertson, of that day, that night; I'd still have her haunting me, I'd still have her voice in my ear. Still have the trauma, the phantom pains. I'd still be impotent ... still broken. So, what was the point of carrying on? What was the point to anything?

I'd been asking myself the same questions too often recently. There was a need to take the entire packet, yet it wasn't easy to put an end to it. To do so was to give up and accept the feeling of shame that went with it. Shame and betrayal. I would be betraying my past: who I was, my parents who had raised me, and the old soldiers who had trained me.

As I lay there waiting for the Zopiclone to kick in, I thought about how much longer life could continue this way, and how difficult it was for a soldier, who has been trained to kill others, to kill himself.

2

March

I woke to the sound of knocking on the bedroom door.
'Chaney, are you dressed?'
'No.'
'Okay, I'll make myself a cup of tea, then. You've got ten minutes to pull yourself together.'

Ten minutes later I was dressed in jogging bottoms and a sweatshirt and was sitting on the edge of my bed when Lorna knocked again, and then walked in to the bedroom. 'Are you feeling a bit better today?'

I wasn't. I was mentally exhausted. I felt as if I'd spent the night back in the abattoir. I didn't feel I could face physio, but I'd successfully avoided the last two sessions. I knew Lorna wouldn't let me get away with another day off.

I nodded.

'Good. Come on, let's start by walking around the cottage.'

After three circuits Lorna said, 'Well, you found that easy enough.'

It was a lie. She knew I'd struggled the entire time, but there was a psychological war going on between us. Lorna was young but the way she plied her trade - physiotherapy - was old school. Her approach was better suited to the army than civilian life. Blind optimism and treating the difficulties I was encountering as trivial were her weapons of choice most days.

'Let's take a short walk down to the beach.' She said.

'I don't think I can manage that.'

'There's only one way to find out. You can hold on to my arm.'

I refused the offer of her arm but managed to limp down to the beach. She was insistent I walk at least a short distance along it. But I refused to move, other than back to the cottage. As soon as we got back I announced that I felt so bad I had to lie down.

That's how it went most days. She would attempt to get me to do more than I was capable of, with me attempting to do less. The end result being a compromise. By getting at least one morning in bed, and there being no visits at the weekend, I ended up doing a lot less than she wanted. In a way it was like being back in prison, where I would watch the lifers win their little victories over the guards – acts of defiance that were so minor the guards could do nothing about them.

*

The following morning was easier. Lorna knew I had a GP appointment, and she drove me up there. She helped me out of the passenger seat, looked me in the eye, and delivered the brief speech that I had known only too well was coming.

'Now, after you see the doctor, try your best to walk home. I know you can do it. Don't let me down and give up. I know you, you're not a quitter.'

As she drove off I couldn't help smile at the irony of what she'd said. She didn't know a thing about me.

The psychological war continued.

*

I sat opposite Dr Rosemarie Grant, and half listened as she summarised the contents of my medical records. Records that she'd only just received, hence the delay in us meeting face-to-face. Under normal circumstances it wouldn't have been long before she reached the serious stuff – post Andorra – except those pages would be missing from the file.

As she was reading, I thought about when I had been in hospital in Barcelona and it had been almost entirely female staff that had looked after me. In military hospital it had been mostly men. Now, it was women again. Doctor, physiotherapist, and carer ... or was it home help? Cook and bottlewasher? There was something about Emily though, that intense sadness, a look that I'd seen before, but couldn't pinpoint.

'It appears that my role here is more of a distributor of medication for you. Everything important that I should know, your past employer – which I assume was the government – feels I don't need to know, other than you are suffering from an extreme form of post-traumatic stress disorder. Should you want to talk about that at any time then I am here for you. I am also here for you in the capacity of GP for your general health. In regard to your medication: in the long term it would be better if you could gradually try to reduce it, but only if you're comfortable doing so.'

She closed my file. 'Now, I understand you're receiving physiotherapy weekdays and you have a carer coming in every day to clean up and make sure you're eating.'

Cook and bottle washer then.

'It's the latter that concerns me. I am sure you're well aware your BMI is significantly below what it should be. How are you getting on with Emily?'

The question caught me by surprise. 'Fine,' I said.

Small town, everyone knows everyone else, nevertheless the familiar way she had used the given name was a little odd coming from a GP. But it was what she said next that really confused me.

'I have your weight on discharge from hospital, and you're down two kilos.' She shook her head. 'Emily has been employed to look after you and get you eating regularly. If you're weight isn't up by the end of next month she'll be replaced ... and frankly, it's better for her if she's working.'

I stared at the woman across from me. This wasn't emotional blackmail to get me to eat? No, there was something else going on here.

*

I slowly limped down the hill towards the high street. My left knee protested, even when I put almost all of my weight on to the walking stick. I went over the last part of the conversation again. Ordinarily I might have expected, 'She needs the work' which would reflect Emily's need for an income that went with employment. But Dr Grant had said, 'It's better for her if she's working.' Doctors are smart cookies, they choose their words carefully. She was telling me something. And that puzzled me.

I had no intention of walking along the high street – far too many people around for someone who wanted to remain anonymous. More importantly, far too many people for someone who's afraid of people. I cut across the street and two minutes later I was on the beach.

Thankfully there were only a handful of people around. A young woman walking her dog, a couple of kids flinging lumps of seaweed at each other. The sand was soft underfoot, which threw me a little off balance, but the real problem was the stick. It was sinking too far into the sand, compounding my loss of balance. This kind of sand may cushion a fall, but I wasn't confident of being able to regain my feet. The thought of lying stranded and helpless flashed through my mind. It was a stupid thought as on this beach it wouldn't be long before someone would be over to help. But that would involve contact with others. I turned to my right - and north - for the harder, damp sand that ran alongside the water's edge.

I liked the feel of the cool breeze against my face. It was midday, or high noon as Jason - my spotter - always called it, and the breeze would be a welcome companion on the half mile trek back to the cottage. My pace was always slow, but today I slowed it down even more, that is until I saw the dark clouds gathering on the horizon. A storm was coming.

Back in the cottage I spent the entire afternoon trying to work out all possible reasons why Dr Grant had made that comment about Emily. There had to be a reason, but everything I came up with seemed highly unlikely. The easy solution would be to go to the local bar, get talking to one of the regulars, and casually throw Emily's name into the conversation. Except that could get me in to a bit of trouble. I was a new face in a small community; if I started asking about one of the local girls, the men could become suspicious and protective. Especially with her being so good looking. The last thing I wanted was to have my name bandied around bars and cafés as being a predator. On top of that, the thought of interacting in a pub was daunting. I wanted to know the reason behind the doctor's comment, though. Perhaps I could just go for a couple of drinks, and let the visit play out. People with a few drinks in them have loose tongues. I was new, they would ask about me, it would be only natural for me to mention my physio and carer. If I felt uncomfortable, I could always leave.

It never occurred to me that, here I was - making a mission of a solitary comment from a doctor. A comment that, in all probability, meant absolutely nothing. Such was my life now, where the slightest thing could quickly become an obsession.

Had my life become so meaningless? Or was it simply about survival? It made sense that the survival part of me might deliberately focus on the most insignificant event and blow it out of proportion to avoid immersing myself in thoughts of suicide.

For today at least, it was working. Tomorrow was too far away to even contemplate.

3

May

I sat at the kitchen table as Emily prepared breakfast for me. 'I didn't manage physio this morning.' I said.
'I know. Lorna's not too happy with you. I realize there's a pain factor, but you really need to try to walk more.'
'I wanted to talk to you about that. I couldn't face exercise early this morning, but I was thinking that after breakfast I might go for a walk. But I'm still a little unsteady on my feet. I don't feel comfortable walking on my own.'
'You want me to walk with you?'
'I'd like that, if you're not busy.'

*

As my carer walked, and I limped along the beach the conversation drifted towards my childhood.
I never liked bringing up the past, going back to a time when emotions ruled, because I usually ended up bringing both my parents' pain, especially my mother. But it seemed natural to talk about it to Emily.
'I was more than a problem child. I was a nightmare for my parents. If something happened in a film or whatever where there was injustice, I would go berserk – to me, what I was seeing on TV was not actors, TV, for me, was another view of reality: I saw it happening in real life. Unable to accept bullying of any kind, group violence towards one person, or any violence towards a woman I would start hitting things, smashing furniture. My father would drag me up to my room, whereupon I would start on the furniture in there. The

beatings he gave me then only made me angrier, as in my twisted logic I saw him siding with the bullies on screen.'

'Why didn't they stop you watching television, ban you from the TV room?'

'They did, eventually, but that didn't stop me behaving the same way at school. Except it wasn't furniture I was breaking. There were fights every week. Most of them were passed off as playground fights or fights that took place down a lane after school. But as I turned older the damage I inflicted resulted in the school hearing about it. With my father working, it was always my mother who had to turn up to see the headmaster. I loved my mum, and I hated seeing her distressed, but no matter how hard I tried I couldn't control my anger. Then everything came to a head with the seagull.'

'*The* seagull?'

'The damned seagull. We lived near the coast and there was a canal behind where we stayed – it was my route for walking home from school. Some days there were swans around, but most days I would see ducks. On this particular day I watched a duck with its young, a solitary duckling, swimming together, the duckling right alongside its mother. Then this seagull swoops down, skims the surface of the water, picks up the duckling, lands on the other side of the canal, two gulps and it's gone. Its mother is beside herself, swimming round in circles calling out for its young.'

'What did you do?'

'The canal was too wide for me to jump across, the bridge too far away. But if I'd managed to get hold of that seagull it would have suffered before it died. I knew what I could do though. I ran home, grabbed a box of pellets and my air rifle and went on a killing spree. I couldn't tell you the number of seagulls I killed that day. If I hit them in the body they were stunned for long enough for me to get to them and club them to death with the butt of the rifle. The few I hit with a headshot, I killed outright.

'I had no idea of how much time had passed, but realized when I saw my father walking home from work. I hot-tailed it to my room, hid the air rifle, took out my school books and pretended I was studying, listening for the slamming of the back door. An hour passed before I heard it slam, followed by his heavy footsteps on the stairs.

'He stood in the doorway, holding the thick leather belt that he kept in a drawer in the kitchen. He then told me that if I lied to him, I would get the beating of my life. He began with telling me he'd spent the last hour picking up, bagging and binning dead seagulls. He asked why I'd killed them. I told him about the canal.

'"Seagulls are known for doing that," he said. "It's life. You need to get used to this sort of thing happening. If you don't, and keep reacting like you have today, you'll spend most of your life in prison. We live in a cruel world, son, and you will have to accept that and adapt to it."

'To my surprise he then asked about the seagulls I hadn't clubbed to death, and had I killed them with a headshot? When I told him that with two of the headshots the birds had been in flight he said, "Right, the fair is on the esplanade this week. They always have air rifle stalls. If you're telling the truth, we'll clean up."

'We went to the fair that evening. And that's exactly what happened. The fair was massive, covered about a mile on the pavement next to the seafront. At one end I won two of the top prizes, then we drove to the other end and won the big prize there. By now word had spread. The next stall I went to they took one look at me, shook their heads and said, "You've won enough sonny. Now fuck off."

'I thought my father would take offence at me being spoken to this way, but he loved it. He loved the fact that these guys, kings of the hustle, had just been hustled by his boy, and they knew it.

'We drove through town, one of the giant stuffed toys I'd won was in the boot, the other was sitting in the back seat alongside me, and the biggest one, a gorilla, was in the front passenger seat with his head and shoulders sticking out of the sunroof. It was a summer evening and the pavements were busy, everyone was smiling or laughing as we drove past. I knew we were going to the children's hospital to hand the cuddly toys in, but I also knew this wasn't the quickest way to get there. Suddenly I realized my father was showing off—showing off what I'd done. It dawned on me, seeing the smile on his face that, for the first time in my life, my father was proud of me.

'I felt like a giant when we walked in to the hospital. I held on to one stuffed toy, my father had one under each arm. I handed the first one over, then he passed the second and third one to me. He made me hand over each one separately. There was a young woman at the reception desk. She was a stunner and she told me how much the children would love them and started asking all these questions. She took my father's lead and spoke directly to me the entire time. "I take it you'll be a marksman then?" she asked.

'As I nodded, my father said, "You're looking at the future best shot in the British Army."

'And that's effectively what happened: from then on my future was dictated by what had started out as one of the worst days of my life, before it turned in to one of the best. I finally began to understand it wasn't so much about controlling my anger, it was having a direction to channel it in. Six months later I turned 16 and joined the Junior Leaders.'

'Junior Leaders?'

'Boy soldiers. When we turn 17 and a half we are moved up in to the regular army. I went to the King's Own Royal Border Regiment – army recruiting offices tend to place you in local regiments – and we'd been living in Whitehaven in west Cumbria since we had left Edinburgh. Boys from Whitehaven had a reputation as fighters; for a lot of us, enlisting in the army was the obvious choice when we left school. I was at home in the Regiment.'

'So, you became a sniper?'

'Yep, within five years I'd won the cup at Bisley, and was awarded the Queen's medal; won just about every shooting competition there was to win.'

We'd stopped now, and we both looked out at the sea and at the waves lapping gently up the beach. A couple of minutes passed in silence, then Emily said quietly.

'Ever wondered what would have happened if you hadn't seen the seagull that day?'

I replied, almost in a whisper, 'No, but I've wondered about a lot of other things.'

That's how it went for the next few weeks: breakfast with Emily. Walk with Emily. The conversations between us were almost always about my past. There was plenty there to talk about, but I was careful not to talk about anything relating to the SAS or my time in prison. She was forming a picture, but it was one I was deliberately projecting. One of someone trustworthy. One of a man who'd lived a fairly full life without anything extreme happening. One of a lie.

I loved our walks - being close to her, talking, sharing fragments of our lives. But I also knew that there was more going on: I was beginning to see her the same way I used to see Charlotte - as a weapon. My desire for Charlotte was the driving force that got me through my time in prison, and after I was released, for getting my life back together. But where the relationship with Charlotte was based on desire, my relationship with Emily was different. I was physically attracted to her for sure - at times I found myself almost spellbound by her natural beauty - and I yearned for some form of physical contact, but that desire was laced with fear, and a vulnerability. What would I do if something did start to happen between us? As much as I was afraid of her finding out by accident, I feared telling her more. I couldn't remember feeling this level of desire to hold a woman before. The irony being there was nothing to follow that desire up with.

As the month drew to a close, Emily began to open up to me more and I began to think I wouldn't have to go into a bar to find out about her. But time passed and nothing of note was forthcoming. I was going to have to try another way. She came up in conversation with Lorna and I casually asked if there was a reason for Emily's sadness. Lorna made eye contact and shook her head. 'Don't go there. You won't like what you find. I know the two of you are getting on okay; don't ruin that by intruding on something that's none of your business.'

The comment, and the way it was delivered, made me want to find out more. To start with, it confirmed there was something there. Something had happened. And now, because there was nothing else in my life, my interest in Emily had suddenly developed into the thing I feared would happen. She had become an obsession.

PART TWO

The Push

4

No one seemed to notice when I hobbled into the bar. I guessed it was my clothing, mostly drab browns or black. At the bar itself I took off my cap and ordered a large Wild Turkey. I turned around and found my eyes darting everywhere, trying to take everyone in at once: the colours, the movement, the noise, the faces. So many people, so little going on, yet so much in the many conversations. My senses were not used to this level of activity. The majority of the tables at the back of the room where I was were full, in direct contrast to the front area, which was effectively empty. I looked around for a chair to sit on. I wasn't going to risk the high stool, so I remained standing at the bar.

I wondered how long I could stand here, waiting for one of the locals to speak to me. The barmaid was always a possibility ... no, not any longer as a giant of a man entered and occupied her attention. He must have been around six foot six and reminded me of someone. I struggled to recall who. He was a lot like the big Argentinian tennis player – but that wasn't who I was thinking of. Physically this guy's shoulders were broader, his waist narrower. Almost inhuman, almost like a caricature, cartoon like ... yes, that was it, Popeye's nemesis: Bluto. I couldn't stop staring at him. When you suddenly see a cartoon character come to life in front of you, it's hard to look away. By the time I realized I should be looking somewhere else it was too late.

Bluto called out, 'What are you looking at, short stuff?'

I glanced behind me as if he'd been speaking to someone else.

'Well, cat got your tongue, short stuff?'

I ignored him, downed the bourbon and using my stick limped round the bar towards the entrance in a wide arc to avoid him.

Out of the corner of my eye I could see him pushing chairs out of the way as he cut across the bar to intercept me. Bluto was coming, that was all I could think. As I neared the door he accelerated, tables and chairs were now flying through the air as he bulldozed a path directly to me. Bluto was charging! The whole situation was bizarre. Here I was, reliving a cartoon from my childhood ... only one thing was missing: I was not Popeye.

I kept moving at the same pace, but I was too slow. He was at my shoulder now. Grabbing my arm he leaned in, and whispered so no one else would hear.

'You smiling at me, gimp? What's your name? Tell me your name.' And I was terrified, because it wasn't his voice I was hearing. It wasn't his breath on the side of my face ... I was no longer in a bar in North Berwick, I was in an abattoir in Andorra and the living nightmare that was Robertson was back with a vengeance.

From behind him the barmaid's voice carried across the room, 'For God's sake, Davey! The man can barely walk.'

Bluto's grip relaxed slightly, but the hate and rage in his eyes remained. 'Aye, she may have saved you this time, gimp, but next time ah see you, you're mine,' he whispered.

The anger that had always surfaced whenever I witnessed the actions of a bully was missing. Fear dominated and without the anger to lead me, I was lost. I focused on putting one foot in front of the other and limped towards the exit.

As soon as I was outside I took in a deep breath of air. How much worse can the day get? I thought, as I limped slowly away, heading in the direction of the beach.

I didn't really know who I was anymore. It was as if, during those 24 hours with Robertson my identity had been blown apart. The fragments that remained were snapshots of my past. Little episodes that I could remember, but my identity, my self-belief, my confidence, had gone. And here I was, almost two years on, with a broken body hunting around trying to find the right bits to stick back together, and it was hopeless, it was pathetic. With people like the Bluto lookalike around, I would never reassemble my life. I would spend the rest of it a victim.

*

It was over an hour since returning to the cottage, and I was still going over what had taken place in the bar – trying to change it, create a past where I had not been cloaked in fear. Why was I there in the first place? Then I remembered I was there to get chatting to the locals in an attempt to find out about my carer. Well, one thing was for certain: I wasn't going to be visiting a bar again, not ever.

I looked across at the laptop. It would be a pointless exercise – there would be nothing on there about Emily but as a process of elimination I had no choice; I had to check. Besides a bit of surfing the net might keep images of what had taken place in the bar from my mind ... at least for a few minutes.

Charlotte used to chastise me for not searching on social media, but the vastness of it frightened me. I liked to have fixed boundaries that I couldn't stray beyond. Google was a trusted compass to guide me across the open expanse of the net. Less than a minute after beginning my search I found myself staring at Emily's name in an article in *The Scotsman,* my curiosity leading me as I raced through the first few lines until I came to an abrupt stop. I paused for a few seconds, readjusting, and continued reading though no longer as someone who knew Emily, but as someone detached, a stranger devoid of emotion. Once I'd finished reading the article through for a second time, I got up from the chair, limped through to the bedroom, sat down on the bed, fell over on to my side and closed my eyes. I needed some form of escape from what I'd just read and all the horrors in the world. Sleep was the nearest I would get to that, and mercifully it took me away from them quickly.

It was the sound of car horn in the distance that woke me. Reality slowly crept in to my world, but it was different, despite there being no whispering from Robertson, it was somehow worse. Last night I'd been able to shut out what I'd read, but this morning, in the cold light of day, emotions were finding a way through my guard. Line of sight – you only really felt the emotion and pain of an event when it involves someone you care about. I began to realize just how much I cared for Emily. As each minute passed, it was not anger I felt growing within me, it was something else. Rage? Fury? Yes and no. Mostly it was a need to act, an overpowering need to do something terrible to a man called Harry Cotton. At the conclusion of his ten-day trial the verdict was 'not proven', which to me meant one thing: he did it, but there was insufficient evidence to secure a guilty verdict. My mind searched around, frantically looking for something to guide me.

A plan. I needed a plan. More precisely, an action plan. I needed more information, though. I went back on to the laptop and brought up the article again, this time noting down the information I needed. I had a letter to post. In the high-tech world of iPhones, Skype, and emails, the old-fashioned letter was by far the slowest, but in my world it was also the most secure way of sending a message.

I would have to go out later and purchase a pay-as-you-go phone. I would use my physio session with Lorna to do that. After writing the mobile number on the foot of the letter, I decided I would post it to John at some point this afternoon.

The last time I'd seen John Waterson was during the briefing for the job in France. The job we were diverted from to take on the capture of Robertson in Andorra. John supplied the intel, as he had done for a number of jobs when I was in the SAS. He was a civilian, yet the ultimate professional. He hadn't been involved in the Robertson mission: there simply hadn't been time. If he had been, it wouldn't have turned out the way it did.

In the evening, after posting the letter to his PO box, I slowly made my way back to the cottage, deep in thought. As I lay in bed that night I began to realize the change that was taking place. I was now having to make decisions: about what actions I should take, and what I should not do. I was certain my old friend would track Cotton down. It wouldn't take John long to build a file on him. Relevant addresses, activities, friends, habits – the works, basically. Within a few weeks I would know everything there was to know about Harry Cotton. I had to do something about this man, but exactly what would be dependent on the info gathered about him. No, it wouldn't depend on that. A not proven verdict was fair game as far as I was concerned. It was more dependent on what I was capable of, or rather, what I could *potentially* be capable of, as right now, I wasn't capable of anything. The events of yesterday being a constant and painful reminder of that fact.

*

The next morning, I woke having been haunted by the usual nightmares but instead of letting them drag me back into the past I closed a shutter on them. In my mind it was a thick, heavy reinforced-steel shutter - like the ones on jewellery stores - and I hauled it down letting its weight build momentum so when it hit the ground it brought a finality: a symbol that I wasn't going to think of anything to do with Andorra for the rest of the day. Within a minute I was sitting upright, my mind engaged in the future as I worked through a number of possible plans of action.

I didn't know what John was going to come up with; however, it was almost certain that I would be required to take some form of physical action. I had enough money to pay to have the job done, but this was personal; I had to do it, which in my current state would point to rifle work. Even if the police conducted a shoddy investigation they would look closely at Emily. She had a strong motive, and that meant everyone she had contact with would be looked at. My new identity was built to allow me to start a new life - it wasn't built to withstand a police investigation. Using a rifle was out, but there was another reason I wasn't going to take that route, a reason that did not involve the police.

This was going to be different from anything I'd been involved in before. To start with, it was not a military operation; I had no team around me, no protection. I looked at it as a hypothetical problem. Whatever version I played out, I required something that would be as effective as an alibi. My physical state gave me exactly that. I just had to get in shape whilst continuing to present the world of North Berwick with that of a disabled man. Lorna would be the biggest problem, yet if I did it right, both her and Dr Grant's statements to the police would eliminate me as a suspect.

Where do I start - upper body, legs? Both. I'd been driving a Land Rover when it went over a mine during the Gulf War, and had spent five months in a rehab hospital. What I went through then would be of greater benefit to me than my most- recent experiences in hospital, but I would have to be careful not to rush things and overtrain. Though, with the pain I would have to subject myself to, would overtraining be a problem? No, the problem would be doing enough to make steady progress. I checked my painkillers. I didn't like using them, but I had plenty if needed. How long would it take to be ready? A year? No, that was too far off ... six months? That would be an optimistic figure, but one I could work towards.

I hadn't even considered the possibility that Cotton might be dead or off-grid. His trial had taken place three years ago, so I should have, but somehow I felt certain that he was alive and still in Scotland. The difference in my attitude was too obvious to ignore, something long dormant inside me had been triggered. I hadn't suddenly woken from a bad dream. Life, reality, sickened me even more; the difference was, this time, I felt I could something about it.

When I was young, I'd read a biography about the famous strongman Joe Greenstein, and how, as a boy, his mentor had told him that before beginning a task he must first succeed in his mind, then the outcome would be irreversible. In the near two years since Andorra, I had achieved absolutely nothing. Considering how much I'd changed since yesterday, it seemed clear that I hadn't forgotten the mentor's words: rather, now, I found myself with a reason to apply them.

PART THREE
The Misdirection

5

June

I was running around the giant storeroom. Each circuit of the room was 112 strides – approximately 112 metres. I'd counted it on the days I'd walked around it. I'd counted it on the days I'd jogged around it. Killing time. But today I was running ... fast. Around and around ... again and again and again. Each time faster than the time before. After more than 50 circuits I was close to sprinting ... the storeroom walls becoming a blur; then I was through them, across the exercise yard, over the prison walls and out. Over the hills and along avenues of trees. Out into freedom and the vastness of the sky. I could hear the wind, feel it beat against my face—

The inmate in charge of the storeroom yelled out, 'Hey Usain! Will you stop doing that. You're making me fuckin' dizzy!'

I was immediately back in the storeroom, back in prison and, on waking fully, back in North Berwick, in a different prison: one where I could no longer run. Yet, with the walks with Emily getting progressively longer, my leg muscles were slowly developing. Was the dream a sign? Was it feasible? If I could overcome the pain, perhaps it was – especially with the beach and soft sand just a few feet away from my back door.

The signs were positive. When I would wake due to a nightmare I would no longer lie in bed allowing memories and thoughts of Robertson to work away at me. Closing the steel shutter on such thoughts had become second nature now, leaving me free to get up and, after warming up, work with Therabands before sets of press-ups between chairs and sit-ups. At first I couldn't manage a single press-up between two chairs, now I could do 12. Charles Atlas had come up with that exercise, along with others, after watching a lion stretching in a zoo. His series of exercises with little or no equipment formed the foundations for his dynamic tension training method. To say it was old school would be an understatement, but it was at the heart of my routine to regain my strength.

I needed to move up a gear, though; I was holding back, and I knew the reason: Lorna. She was good at her job, no matter how well I camouflaged it, she would eventually notice the change.

It was time to see my GP.

*

A week later I was sitting at the kitchen table, while Emily made a breakfast of kippers. She glanced over and said, 'I spoke with your GP yesterday. She asked me if I wanted to take over the job of physio. She said she felt you responded better to me than to Lorna.' As Emily finished speaking she stopped what she was doing and turned to face me.

'Well, I do,' I said. 'And I told the doctor exactly that. I'm not making any progress with Lorna. It's not her fault, it's just that it's not an effort with you. I enjoy our walks together.'

'You know I'm not trained. Lorna's the expert. She knows what you need. I don't.'

'I've been here before, Emily. Years ago I was in an accident and spent several months in hospital learning to walk again. I went through it all. All the different things that the physios subjected me to, what I responded to and what I didn't. I had no choice then, but now it's different. Dr Grant told me that you're not employed by the NHS; you're paid by my previous employer.'

'The NHS wouldn't provide you with the level of home care you currently receive. And I'm quite sure they will be more than happy if they can move Lorna onto other patients.'

'But are you okay with taking on my physio?'

'Only if we can improve on what you're currently doing.'

'Minimum two miles by the end of the year. Two walks a day, a mile each walk.'

Emily nodded, 'I think your old employer should be happy with that.'

'They are happy that my weight is coming up, and that's down to you. So, we're set, then: you can let Lorna loose on other patients?'

'All right, let's try it and see how it goes. I'll let Dr Grant know later today. She will contact the physiotherapy department. Lorna might be here for one more session, but that'll be it.'

Things were going to plan. With Lorna out of the way, I could step up my exercise routine in private. The two walks would mean more time alone with Emily; and with that, more time for trust to develop, and for her to open up about the past. When the dreams woke me during the night, I could go out on to the beach, try a slow jog, no doubt fall over, pick myself up and try again.

With the dreams of Robertson no longer dominating my life, I now knew the answer to the broken soldier question.

6

July

The summer was a hot one, which was unusual for Scotland. Normally May is the sunniest month, the summer itself being broken up in to a few hot days here and there throughout June, July and August.

To avoid the midday heat the walks with Emily now took place earlier; sometimes even before breakfast, and always around sunset. In addition to my newly found direction, and the positive feedback from my slowly developing exercise routine, I now had something to look forward to towards the end of the day. The evening walks were precious to me and if we walked east along the beach we could watch the sunset on the way back. The weeks passed, our conversations developed, I confided in her more and more, but I would always fall short of telling her about the time I spent in the SAS. In turn she opened up about a number of things, mostly from her childhood. It may have been deliberate, it may have been an unconscious decision, but so far she had told me nothing about her daughter. If I hadn't seen *The Scotsman* article, I wouldn't have known she'd had a child.

At the end of the month, the peace of the summer was broken by John's visit. Around 6pm I heard a knocking on the back door. I recognized the sequence and welcomed my old friend into the kitchen. I quickly called Emily and cancelled our evening walk. While I made coffee, John began his report.

'A few months after the not proven verdict Cotton moved to Alnwick. He doesn't work as such, lives comfortably off the interest from a substantial inheritance. He dabbles in the stock market and has financial interests in a number of small businesses. He associates with three other men around the same age and social standing.' John summarised their backgrounds and occupations.

'This is where it turns ugly.' He looked directly at me and said very quietly. 'All four have money and they have the indestructibility of youth. They think that there's nothing they can't do. Hurting people is a game to them. And it's one of their favourites. Murder, however, is not. The murder in the not proven verdict relating to Cotton, was not premeditated; things simply got out of control.'

'Were they all involved?' I asked.

John lowered his eyes. 'All of them were involved.'

'Did the police suspect the involvement of the three friends?'

'Not from the information I was able to obtain.'

The hesitation that then followed on his part was a clear indication of the conflict he was in. Shaking his head, John pulled from his inside pocket what looked like a mobile phone, but transpired to be a small video camera.

'On Friday evenings they all meet at a converted farmhouse three miles outside Alnwick. I found a handful of recordings at the farmhouse. I copied one. You don't get a good look at any of the men's faces in it, though it's clear to me who they are. I'll leave it with you, but you really don't want to see it. You can destroy the file and the camera now or after you've seen it. As your friend I advise you to destroy it now. I'm through in Glasgow tomorrow. Do you have anyone coming round in the morning?'

'Emily. She'll be here around eight.'

'I'll be here at seven.'

With that he was gone, leaving the pocket video camera on the kitchen table.

*

Two hours later and the camera still lay on the kitchen table. I knew what I was doing. Trying to distance myself from the footage that was on it.

Eventually I picked it up, held it in my hands for a minute. Then, after checking both front and back doors were locked, I sat down at the kitchen table and watched the footage.

After watching I deleted the file. I took it outside, placed it on a paving stone, and took a hammer to it. Then started a small fire at the bottom of the garden. I threw the shattered remains of the camera onto the fire, adding bits of wood, carboard, plastic, and anything from the rubbish bin that burned. I stood a couple of feet back and watched the red glow of the sunset in the distance. I could feel the warmth of the fire on my face.

John had warned me. Why hadn't I listened?

I have to face Emily tomorrow. I shook my head. How was I going to do that? At least she didn't know anything about the film. One thing I had to make sure of: she wouldn't learn of its existence.

Not ever.

*

John arrived at precisely seven in the morning; I hadn't slept. Instead, I'd pulled a plan together on the information I'd been given. My friend took one look at me and knew that

I'd seen the footage. He took the shopping list I'd written out for him, looked it over and said quietly, 'You know, although they've been careful to keep their faces out of shot, with the other films there's more than enough evidence in that farmhouse to have all four locked up for years—'

He looked at me, shook his head and added, 'Sorry, I wasn't thinking. I, of all people, should know you'll need to deal with this your way.' He went back to studying the list. 'I can get all of this in Glasgow. I'll drop them off this evening.'

I nodded. After he left I called Emily again, explaining I had had a bad night and I would miss breakfast and see her for our evening walk.

I lay down on the bed and closed my eyes. I had ten hours to lock the footage from that video away in the darkest recess of my mind.

7

August

John had been busy. After going over my plan with him, when he was back down south, he filmed footage of the farmhouse and the four men meeting there on a Friday evening. They all came in their own cars, generally all relatively punctual, arriving at intervals over a 15 minute period. Only the first to arrive had to unlock the front door. He then left it ajar for the others.

To make sure I got all four, I needed to hit all of them on the same evening. With them arriving separately I could take them one at a time as they walked into the main room. John warned me that I might have to deal with two at once – though this, he figured, would be unlikely.

That still left it as a possibility, so I had to be in good enough shape to fight two men. I would have to move my exercise routine up another gear.

August passed with me half jogging, half running west along the beach at night, always having most of my face covered with the hooded top of my sweatshirt. It was in complete contrast to the side I showed the town during daylight hours. The walks along the beach were gradually increasing in length, though they remained painfully slow, with me leaning heavily on my stick and deliberately dragging my left leg. With Emily walking alongside, we presented the public with a very authentic view of a disabled man and his carer. Our walks together took in the full length of the beach to the east, up to and beyond the harbour. The deception was working perfectly, even Emily didn't know it was going on.

However, time was passing with her still failing to say anything about her daughter. I felt a need to tell her that Cotton was still abusing children, and the action I planned to take. As my strength steadily increased, so did that need. I would be ready soon, and when I was, I wanted to move quickly. These men needed to be stopped before they ruined any more lives.

I knew I didn't have to tell Emily anything. I could just do it and tell her afterwards, but if she believed she was making the decisions, she might accept she at least played a part in Cotton's death. Feeling that would hopefully give her some sense of closure.

8

September

After breakfast, as we sat at the kitchen table, Emily commented that, as it was such a lovely day, we should take a walk along to the harbour.

I nodded, but I wasn't thinking of the walk. I was debating whether this was the best time to bring up her daughter. It had become clear she wasn't going to do it so it was up to me. In the end I reasoned that there was no best or good time. It was always going to be a bad time. Now was as bad a time as any.

'True story,' I said, getting Emily's attention. 'An experienced climber takes a bad fall on a mountain, shattering his leg. Then that night, during a snowstorm he falls again and finds himself halfway down a crevasse. He wasn't strong enough to climb to the surface, so he worked his way down to the bottom. From there he had no way of knowing which direction to take, but he chose one and slowly made his way to the end of it. As he broke out in to daylight he was greeted by snow and ice. He knew the direction of base camp, but he also knew that to get there he had to cross many miles of broken jagged rocks. With his shattered leg, hungry, exhausted, and dehydrated he set out to cross the rocks, all the time aware that even if he managed to reach base camp, the likelihood was that no one would be there.'

'Okay, and why are you telling me this?'

'Despite the apparent impossibility of survival, he kept making decisions. He kept moving forwards.'

'And?' She looked at me and shrugged her shoulders.

'What are you going to do?'

'Do? Do about what?'

'Do about the man responsible for your daughter's death.'

Stony silence. She stood and walked to the window.

'Who've you been talking to? Was it Lorna?'

'Lorna lives and breathes physiotherapy. If I'd asked her a question that was unrelated to that subject she would have probably slapped me.' I shook my head. 'I didn't need to ask anyone. I knew something was wrong. I googled your name and North Berwick. So, back to my original question, what are you going to do?'

She switched back to the story, almost as if the last part of the conversation hadn't taken place, 'Tell me, did he make it to base camp?'

'Yes.'

'And were there people there?'

'Yes.'

'Great story, just one little hiccup – I am not a fucking mountain climber! I am a mother who had her child raped and murdered and you cannot possibly begin to comprehend the emotions I feel! The courts know who did it, but they let him go because of lack of evidence.'

'I know about the not proven verdict.' I said. 'The law is effectively saying to him, we're letting you go free, but don't do it again.' I looked at her; tears were streaming down her face.

'Why are you putting me through this?' she said.

'I want to know what you are going to do about it!' I shouted. 'You know, when I look at you I see a life destroyed; I see pain during the day, and nightmares when it's dark. That's not a life.'

Emily glared at me and shouted back 'Those are exactly the things I see when I look at you! You are pathetic, making me go in to this again. I was coping, I was handling things. I was living.'

'No you weren't. You're going through the motions of life, but you're not living. You're in pain. It's been written all over your face since the first moment I laid eyes on you.'

She shook her head, stared at me, then screamed in frustration. 'I don't even know where he is now ... stay away from me! Whatever happened to you has driven you mad. I won't be back. Stay out of my life.'

She turned and was at the back door. As she opened it, I called out.

'Cotton's in Alnwick.'

Emily stopped for a second as she was going through the door. She didn't turn around.

'Stay away from me,' she said with a finality that shook me. Then she was gone.

I opened my eyes, immersed in the feeling that goes with knowing something terrible has happened. Then the guilt penetrated. Then the sense of doom. I had to apologize, go round to where she lived right now and apologize. As I began to get dressed I realized it wouldn't make much of a difference; she wouldn't return to be my carer, but at least I could explain the reason behind my actions. If I could do that then she might hate me a little less. I tied the laces of my trainers and was through the back door and halfway across the porch when I realized how dark it was ... and quiet; the beach was completely empty. I looked at my watch: it was the middle of the night. Then slowly, gradually, somewhere amidst the emotional trauma a sense of hope grew ... had I been dreaming? Was this nothing more than a dream?

It took a further five minutes for me to fully surface and accept that's all it had been – a bad dream.

Having experienced just how upset I had been when I thought I'd hurt Emily brought to an end the frustration and angst I had been feeling. From that morning on I determined to wait until she mentioned her daughter. Only then, and only if it felt right to do so, would I bring up Cotton.

9

They call it an Indian summer, though I'd never been interested enough to find out why. As September neared its end, the sun became hotter. Emily was wearing white shorts and a grey T shirt. I wore an oversized denim shirt hanging loose over a pair of black Canterbury Uglies that were also too big for me. I was into loose clothing now. I had no choice: the previous months of training had developed too much muscle to have on open show. Had I required endurance I would have been able to keep the muscular development to a minimum, but this job required short bursts of explosive strength. I may not have looked like a top athlete, but the size and definition on my shoulders, arms and legs did not correspond to that of a disabled man. A man who is seen regularly hobbling along the beach, leaning heavily on a walking stick, with a carer by his side.

The beach was busy, there were a lot of young children out, building sandcastles, playing football with their friends or parents. The noise of screams of joy and giggling that rang out were typical of a holiday resort. Not many people in the water, though - it wasn't that hot, this was Scotland after all.

'Why don't you ever wear shorts?' Emily asked, looking at my tracksuit bottoms.

'I'm old fashioned.'

She turned to me with a puzzled expression. 'What do you mean? What has being old fashioned got to do—'

She suddenly stopped speaking. She wasn't the only one. The half dozen or so people around a young girl - a child maybe five or six years old - fell silent as the girl broke through the laughter and screams of joy with her own scream: far louder, and one of pain and distress.

When the tide had gone out, along with the odd crab and lengths of seaweed that remained on the sand there was a jellyfish, which, trapped in a shallow pool, hadn't been seen by the girl who had run right through it. Wearing a swimming costume, her leading leg had been badly stung, and she cried out again and again for her mum.

Emily looked away, and said softly, 'My daughter did the exact same thing on nearly the same spot, but she didn't call for me. She didn't cry, she didn't say anything, just showed me the raw redness and swelling of the sting. She was always like that; fell out of tree and broke her arm, never cried. I said to her after it had been x-rayed and we waited for the cast to be put on, "You do know, Ailsa, that it's not just children who cry when their arm is broken, adults cry too." She looked at me and shook her head, "Not soldiers, they don't cry. And I'm going to be a soldier." I have no idea where that determination came from, but when I think back now I can't remember a time when it wasn't there.'

'As tough as a nickel steak.' I said without thinking.

Emily spun her head round to look at me. 'That was her ... yes, that was her – as tough as a nickel steak.'

The opening was there to ask about Emily's use of the past tense, and hope that she would explain, but I wasn't going to risk her sidestepping the issue. Instead, I looked at her and said quietly, 'I know about your daughter. I know what happened.'

The bereft mother wiped away the tears that were pooling, catching them just before they spilled over. She shook her head. 'I imagine you'll know, then, that the man who killed her walked away from the courtroom a free man. Not proven, that was the verdict, and for all I know he's doing the same thing to other children.'

'I know all about Cotton, I know things that the police don't know—'

'How could you possibly know? You've been here the whole time, all you can know is what you've read on the net.'

'When I told you I was in the army there was something I left out. I was SAS – almost everything I was involved in was off the record. Covert operations ... that kind of stuff. We had this contact, a specialist who supplied much of our intel. He was a computer expert. He was also an expert at entering buildings and leaving them without anyone knowing he'd been there. He collected the information. Not long after I arrived here I asked him to get me information on Cotton. A month or so ago he visited and gave me what he'd collected. I know where Cotton lives. I know who his friends are, and where they live. I know where they operate, and where they meet. I know everything.'

She looked down then turned and began walking in the direction of her home. 'I have to go.'

I watched her walk away for a few minutes then turned and limped back to the cottage. With the emotions involved, it was far too much information for her to process. But no matter how I broke it to her, it was always going to be too much.

*

I didn't know when she'd be back, just that she would be. I'd told her I knew everything so she would need to find out exactly what that was. She wouldn't be able to stop herself.

When she did return the next day I was standing outside on the porch, looking out at the water.

'I have questions,' she said.

'I have answers,' I replied.

'You're no longer in the army?'

'Not for years.'

'Then how do you still know this man, the information provider?'

'We have a long-established method of contact through a PO box.'

'How long did it take him to collect the information?'

'Two months. He does have other things to do.'

'And he would do this for you – why?'

'It's complicated.'

'Make it simple.'

'He owes me a favour.'

'Some favour for two months' work.'

I turned to face her. I'd already thought this through. From now on she would get nothing but the truth ... with one exception.

'A group of men, gangsters, threatened his family. It was nothing to do with John, it was his brother. He liked a bet too much, and owed these guys a lot of money. I sorted it.'

'You paid them off?'

I looked out to sea again. I had to cast my mind back to over a decade ago.

'John's brother was lying low. When these guys couldn't find him, they decided to target his immediate family. They went to John's home when he was out, went around the back and walked in through the patio doors. His wife was in the kitchen. They got hold of her and held a knife to her throat. Typical threat and intimidation. To them this was tame, a gentle threat. But the debt became irrelevant the moment they laid their hands on her.'

'What about the other men in your unit, were they involved?'

'I'd met John's wife, I knew his children. He was my friend. I needed to deal with this myself.'

Emily was about to ask a question, but instead paused for a few seconds. Then said, 'How do you know the information about Cotton is accurate?'

'Lives depend on the information John collects. People in high places trust him. I trust him. You should as well.'

'Okay ... he's doing this to return a favour. Why are you doing it? Why are you getting involved? There has to be a reason other than your overactive sense of justice.'

I looked at her. 'You're asking a lot of questions.'

'Yes, and you started it. You delved right in to the heart of my life, most of which is strewn over the internet. Are you telling me I'm not allowed to know about this area of your life?'

Seconds passed, slowly, with me looking at the ground.

Of course she was right, but I hadn't considered she would look this closely at my own past.

'A year ago, I was part of a five-man team sent into Andorra on a capture mission. It was last minute; there should have been another two teams involved but they figured that having the element of surprise would be enough. What we didn't know was that the target was setting us up. She killed the rest of my team; I was the last one breathing, so I was the one she tortured. She worked on one hundred points of my body at the same time. I thought I could handle most pains, but I was naive.

'It wasn't only my joints she worked on with needles. She targeted all the vulnerable areas, all the sensitive areas.' I stopped for a few seconds. 'Those needles left me impotent. Not that big a deal: I'm still alive, that's the main thing.'

I paused again. In the end it had been easy to tell her about the impotence. Now I was left wondering why I'd made such a big deal of it.

'The pain and the memory of what took place has a habit of waking me in the middle of the night. Until recently I would lie awake afraid ... of the dark, afraid that I would hear her whispering in my ear again.' I turned away and looked out to sea, shaking my head I spoke quietly. 'Afraid of everything.'

Emily was about to speak but I asked the question.

'What do you do with a broken soldier?'

'What?'

'I overheard two psychologists discussing my case, deciding my future. The senior one asked the question. Both of them agreed there was nothing you could do.'

I looked across at Emily, she remained silent.

'They were wrong. What do you do with a broken toy soldier?' I asked.

She replied hesitantly, 'You stick him back together again—'

'And put him back on the battlefield,' I said. 'It's the same for a soldier. Psychologists don't understand the mentality within certain branches of the military. You put field dressings on his wounds and send him out to fight again.'

'Send him where? There are no conflicts going on right now, and you're in no condition to go to war if there were.'

'The true soldier will adapt, he will find another battle to fight. He will find another mission.'

Emily didn't reply for almost a minute.

'So I'm the mission?' she said.

'Harry Cotton is the mission.'

'You're going to set him up, make sure there's enough evidence this time?'

'Barely seven per cent of murder, rape, and violence cases reported to the police result in a conviction. The law failed you, yet you want to trust it again. How effective was the law in dealing with Savile? How many children did the law - the system - fail? Did you know that a young man who had been found guilty of raping a 13-year-old was given community service? A jury found him guilty, yet he was allowed to walk free. There's no deterrent there, none. Instead, it's a signpost to young men saying rape away, though you might have to do some menial tasks for a few days for ruining the lives of those girls - not to mention the lives of their families. On top of that catastrophic failing in the Scottish legal system, too many people with connections remain untouchable. I don't care what contacts Cotton has, none of it matters because if he is convicted and given a custodial sentence, the law will still protect him. It would put him in a special unit away from ordinary prisoners. Extra money being spent on him and others like him that could have gone to help build hospitals. The law protects him because of his so called "human rights". Anyone that abuses children loses those rights. They are inhuman, they are monsters. There's only one way to deal with monsters. But before I kill him—'

'Stop!' Emily stared at me in disbelief, then walked over to the other side of the porch. She stood unmoving, looking out, perhaps at something, perhaps at nothing. 'Kill ... really? I'm not going to get involved in killing, I am not like you. I care for people: you kill them. What if you're caught, then we'll both go to prison. I'll be branded a murderer, they'll think I paid you to kill them. Besides the justice system has learnt and moved on since Savile.'

'Has it? Are you sure about that? Family, close friends, what do they do when their loved ones' lives are destroyed? Nothing. Because their lives are destroyed as well. Parents just like you – their lives are ruined. Taking the law into their own hands may cross their mind but the stigma of being branded a killer stops them.'

'I'm not sure about the killing. I need to think.'

With that she left. She returned at her usual time, but the subject was not raised again until a few days later.

*

As we walked along the beach, Emily asked about my being tortured.

'You said "one hundred points of pain"?'

'Exactly one hundred. It was a figure that prompted a discussion amongst the doctors.'

She shook her head.

Her reaction puzzled me. It was almost a form of denial. 'What is it?' I asked.

'Ailsa's favourite book, the main character was tortured on a machine that administered pain to 100 points of his body at the same time.'

'What's the title of the book?'

'Does it matter?'

'Not to me, but I know someone who might be interested.'

As Emily gave me the title, I made a mental note to email the details to Anderson.

She had other things on her mind. 'The killing: I take it you're going to use a rifle.'

'I never considered that. You kill a man at long range, he doesn't know he's going to die. One second he's breathing and life is good, the next second life no longer exists. Take the average man on the street and the most profound event in his life and multiply that by a million and you'll begin to have an idea of the impact that knowing he is about to die will have on him. When you're young it's the utter despair of the reality, the unthinkable that no film or book can convey. The shocking enormity of the finality of it all, your entire world, everything will cease to exist. And that the rules, the logic, the limitations you've lived your life to didn't actually exist – and only existed in your mind because you created them. When you reach that understanding you start to see the colossal potential that you had, and so much of it was wasted on trivial matters.

'Cotton is going to feel that despair, and he'll feel pain. But not just pain: pain that will break his mind, make him wish that he had never lived. He is going to suffer before I kill him.'

'I thought you were just going to kill him, now you're going to torture him first. Why so much hatred for someone you don't even know? To avenge my Ailsa?'

'You can't avenge what was done to Ailsa. Cotton committed the worst crime, against an innocent little girl. I don't feel anything towards him. I feel what I have to do, nothing else. I have a moral duty to protect the children he may harm in the future.

'If only we could break the stigma that goes with "avenging" harm caused to a child. Right now killing a person who has murdered your child is linked closely to revenge, and revenge is generally viewed with condemnation. Break that stigma and the child rapists and murderers in this world will realize the law won't always be around to protect them - that the days are gone when the worst that could happen to them was to be found guilty and incarcerated but, at the same time, put into a special unit, away from the general prison population. They're not afraid of that, but they suddenly become very afraid when they realize that the worst that can happen is to be hunted down, tortured and butchered by members of the child's family. That fear might lead them to find an alternative to molesting and raping chil—'

Emily cut in, 'Then those family members end up spending years, probably decades in prison.'

'Only if they're caught. But even if they are they'll have done something. They will have decided not to live and die a victim. Setting an effective deterrent means brutal measures often have to be taken.'

'I can't have anything to do with this, I am not made like you - I wouldn't survive in prison.'

'I would tell the police you knew nothing about it. I am sure they would believe me if I told them about my previous jobs. Or I could simply tell them I wanted to do this for you because I was in love with you.'

She didn't have time to process what I'd just said as I immediately went on to explain that, while the law protects convicted paedophiles, four out of five reoffend shortly after their release. The government knows this yet they still shorten their sentences - often by half or more - for good behaviour. Emily, however, wasn't interested.

'I just want to forget about it. I'm not going to let you do this.' She said.

'Cotton destroyed your daughter's life. And in destroying her life, he destroyed your life. Yes, I know you don't care about your life, you would gladly give it for Ailsa to have one more chance at life without such a terrible thing having happened to her. You don't care about yourself, you only cared about your child. But what about all the other children that Cotton is going to abuse and harm? What about all the lives that are going to be destroyed? All the children and all the mothers, who, if they could see what was going to happen to their child, would be on their knees begging you to get involved to stop it from happening, to change the future. If you were one of those mothers, you would do anything to save your daughter ... you would sell your soul.'

I was looking directly at her, and saw the tears spill over and hit her cheekbones before falling on to her blouse.

As she turned away and began slowly walking towards her home I called out to her, 'This isn't about revenge. It has nothing to do with you or your child. You can never avenge Ailsa for what he did to her. All you can do is protect other children, and stop them from being harmed, by stopping him.'

From her body language I knew I had her. I should have hated myself for the emotional blackmail, but there was no getting away from it, Cotton and his friends needed to die.

*

I had decided the raid would take place in a fortnight. I'd been over everything numerous times. I was ready. Yet for all the training, the press-ups, sit-ups, working with a four-pound stone hammer and running along the beach in the middle of the night, there was still one thing that had to be done. One more test. Not against walls of sand or a makeshift punch bag, but against flesh and blood, something that moved ... something big.

As much as I would have liked to, I couldn't use the hammer. Aside from its use here being linked to the raid a fortnight later, it would inflict too much damage to avoid a police investigation. That meant using my fists, which I was okay with except I couldn't risk broken knuckles. If I injured my hands that would put the raid back several months. I briefly considered getting a pair of knuckle dusters, but while they wouldn't inflict the same level of damage as a stone hammer, using them might trigger a police investigation. Besides I needed to fight on equal terms, having an unfair advantage would make the whole exercise pointless.

In the spare room I emptied out the contents of my old kit bag. NI gloves were easy enough to spot with their raised section across the knuckle area. I carefully cut through the stitching at one end and withdrew the rectangle of foam padding. I replaced it with the same sized section of tin foil. I was surprised to find I needed almost an entire roll of tin foil for both gloves. Layered and compressed, the two blocks of foil slid neatly into the sections, raising them again. A few strips of black carpet tape secured them in place. And the gloves were ready.

*

Everyone knew where my target lived: alone with his dogs, the end house of the row that ran along the sea front, south of the town. That Thursday evening was the one I'd been waiting for. It was cloudy, and with no moon or stars providing light you could see nothing along the sea front. At midnight I waited at the rear of his house alongside the garage. I wore loose-fitting jeans and a US Air Force green bomber jacket which, bloused and padded made me appear almost ten kilos heavier. When I heard the car pull in to the driveway I donned a black balaclava, then pulled on the NI gloves.

Alone, at night, a normal person would be shocked, or at least surprised, to be confronted by a figure in a balaclava. Not this guy, he laughed out loud.

'Not seen one of 'em for a while. If it's a disguise, it's not going be much use when I take it off you. Is it now?'

I had planned what I was going to do, move straight in and put him down before he had a chance to settle. That he appeared to have settled already didn't change things. As I walked towards him I raised my gloved hands, showing the open palms towards him first, then turning the backs of the hands towards him before balling them into fists. That was not planned, and took me by surprise, and right then, at that moment, I became the man I'd been pretending to be. *I was Chaney* and everything after that involved no conscious thought whatsoever. My right leg snapped out in a perfect front kick, the steel toe of my size 9 Cats, connecting with the soft part of his groin, so hard that if he'd been a smaller man it would have probably lifted him off the ground. As he grunted in pain I launched a right hook, which hit him flush on the lower part of the jaw. He went down like he'd been poleaxed. I was on him, dropping to my knees I hit him a further three times on the side of the jaw. I could see he was unconscious but I wasn't done. His head lay to the side, with my left hand I turned it upwards until he faced me, then drove a straight right in to his mouth. Of the five punches I hit him with, this one - driving straight down with my body weight behind it - was the most brutal. The impact of the blow was so great he regained consciousness. He turned his face to the side, spurting out a mouthful of blood and teeth. By this time I had regained my feet. I walked away, straight down to the beach, found my rucksack, into which I stuffed the gloves, balaclava and bomber jacket. I slipped the hood up on my sweatshirt and then jogged back the mile to the cottage along the waterline.

*

Two days later I heard a strange noise from the kitchen. I went through to find Emily humming. I couldn't make out the tune, but it sounded familiar.

'You seem to be in good mood.' I said.

'I am. I've just heard the local bully boy has been given a long-awaited lesson in manners. It appears three of our young tearaways have finally given him a beating he won't forget. Police picked them up, but they all apparently have very convenient alibis. They broke Davey Kane's jaw in three places and knocked out most of his front teeth. The top row – four of them - all sheared off at the gum line. You won't know him, but he's hated in this town. It's about time he got what he deserved.'

'Maybe it's a good omen?'

'Maybe,' Emily said, with the faintest of smiles.

'That's the first time I've seen you smile. Maybe that's a good omen as well.'

She nodded, 'Maybe.'

*

It was late in the evening, two days before the raid. We'd walked to the west end of the beach and we sat on the sand looking out to sea.

Emily's mood was totally different, and when she spoke her determination was evident.

'You may be ready for this, but I don't think your pretence of being a disabled man is going to hold up anymore. I can see the muscle on you now. It's not going to work. They'll look at the victim. The not proven verdict against Cotton makes me automatically the number one suspect. They'll look into the backgrounds of everyone I am, and have been, in contact with. I don't know your birth name. To me, you're Chaney, but if they are going to check on you they'll probably find out your old name, and your military record. If I wanted revenge, you would be precisely the person I would go to. There's nothing to be gained in continuing with this. It's not going to work.'

I'd anticipated Emily having last minute doubts about the raid.

I said, 'I didn't tell you about this before because Cotton's friends weren't involved in what happened to your daughter, but they've been involved in a lot of other bad stuff. Terrible stuff.'

'How many friends?'

'Three. And I'm not going to going down there to kill just one man. I am going there to kill all four.'

'You're serious? Four? That will make for a huge police investigation—'

'It was always going to be a huge investigation, but at least now, you won't be the number one suspect. Someone else will be.'

'I don't understand ... who will be?'

'Remember the girl I told you about. She was from a military family. Trained for combat from the age of five.

Started uni, apparently rejecting her training and, to all intents and purposes, starting a new life. Then, by chance—'

'You're talking about the girl who tortured you?'

'Right, and it was by pure chance that she was exposed to a military program.'

'You mean like a computer program.'

'Yea, kind of. But there was a problem: the program was flawed; all the other test subjects went insane and then killed themselves.'

'Except her?'

I nodded. 'Opinions differ, but the senior psychologist I spoke to felt the girl's ability to survive was due to her fulfilling the destructive aspect of the program.'

'Which was?'

'Counter-terrorism.'

'Killing terrorists?'

'More than that. The program was particularly aggressive in nature. It was designed to terrorise terrorists. That meant torture, killing, defiling the bodies – Genghis Khan stuff. But it appeared she had a very liberal definition of a terrorist – anyone she saw as a threat to survival she classed as a legitimate target. Industrialists who refused to take measures to protect the environment ended up being tortured and killed. When she realized she was being tracked, she set up a trap. I've already told you about this. She killed the others, tortured me until I gave her the information on who sent us, left me for dead, and went to our base in London where she killed everyone in the building. The sole survivor, who she also left for dead, thinks the girl has somehow manipulated the program and is on some sort of mission to save the world. Thinks the girl believes that global warming and the imminent end of the human race is too big for the mind to handle, resulting in mass denial ... that the path to breaking the denial is by demonstrating the violence that will occur when the major crops fail and law and order ends.'

'What do you think?'

'I try not to think about her. But I don't think anyone really knows what went on in her mind, though the psychologist I saw probably came the closest. He believes that with the girl having been trained to kill from childhood, exposure to the counter-terrorism program merely let her off the leash. Whilst she was committing an act of pure carnage at the department in London she learnt that twenty SAS were searching for her on a tiny island in the Outer Hebrides. So she travelled north, took the next ferry to the island and attacked them. They thought they were hunting her, but it was the other way round. Two of the twenty survived. They stated that they shot her twice at long range before she fell off the edge of a cliff into the Atlantic. Officially she's dead, but there is no body. The two SAS survivors left the army within a month of this incident and went off grid. That they did, casts doubt on the accuracy of their report. They think she could still be alive and they want to be somewhere she won't find them. If she is alive, she has to kill, to inflict pain, to harm. She needs targets. When she doesn't have any targets available, she creates them. Throughout Europe, she went out most nights to the worst bars – nightclubs so populated by criminals that off duty police avoid them. Just by going to these places she was enticing men to attack her as she strolled back to wherever she was staying.

'She has a hatred of rapists, sex offenders of any kind. If the men were on their own when they attacked her, she crippled them. If there were two or more, she would kill them, but she crippled them first. She shattered their joints with a stone hammer. In her two years travelling around Europe, there were over a dozen occasions when she was attacked. Considering that the majority of times the men attacked in twos and threes, made for a hell of a lot of dead bodies.'

'Stone hammer. Like a sledgehammer?'

'No, you need two hands for a sledgehammer. Stone hammers are at most only four inches longer than your normal hammer, but the heads are four times heavier. They're used by stone masons. What you hit, you break. Hit a man hard on the head he'll be dead before he reaches the ground.'

'So this is about making the girl who tortured you – who might be dead – into a suspect.'

I nodded. 'It will divide the resources of the investigators, meaning a lot fewer man-hours spent looking at people like you.'

'Okay, so you're going to use one of those hammers. That's a lot of weight, I don't—'

The weight won't be a problem. Though there is an alternative. Three men tried to rape her in a flat in London. They were found dead, their groins had been cut out and placed alongside the bodies. It was a carbon copy of how slaughtermen cut out an abscess or cancerous growth from cattle, leaving it alongside the carcass for the health inspector's decision as to whether to condemn the entire beast. I could always—'

'I think you should go with the hammer.'

'I think so.'

We sat in silence for a while.

'It was you, wasn't it?' Emily said softly.

'What was me?'

'Davey Kane, it was you. The three lads, their alibis were all genuine. But on the night it happened you cancelled our evening walk. Then when I arrived in the morning I noticed the remnants of a little bonfire you'd had in the garden. I'm now guessing that was the clothes you wore, which probably had blood on them.'

'How long have you known?'

'I had a suspicion, but when you started talking about using a hammer to kill four men, I remembered you telling me about your friend. You never told me what you'd done to the gangsters who threatened his wife. But I know now what you did. The life you used to lead has suddenly become very real. Compared to what you're used to doing, what you did to Kane was nothing more than a cuff around the ear.'

She shook her head slowly, as if suddenly realizing how naive she'd been. After a long pause she continued, 'Anyway, there are a lot of people who would like to thank you for what you did to Kane, myself included. He's a big strong man, but then I'm sure, as ex-army, you're accustomed to ambushing ... especially as the last thing you'd have wanted was for him to see your face.'

There was nothing to be gained by correcting her, besides all four targets were going to be ambushed.

'Still, with his size and strength it was a bit of a risk, wasn't it? Or were you that sure you could beat him?'

'It was a risk, but one I felt I had to take. With Cotton and his friends the plan is to take them one at time; but there's always the possibility I might have to handle two at once. I had to make sure I was ready.'

'I can't talk you out of this, can I?'

I shook my head.

'Then I'm coming with you.'

'No.'

'Yes. You might get hurt and be unable to drive back. I can drive us home.'

'I'll be okay to drive.'

'You don't know that. Maybe you'll be okay to drive but not well enough to avoid being pulled over by the police. I need to drive. I need to be involved. I need closure on this, and the only way I might get that is by seeing Cotton after you've finished with him: seeing him dead.'

'No.'

'I would stay well out of the way until it was over. I would wait for your call before approaching. And even if you drove back, that I was there in case you got hurt would mean I was involved, and that would be a good thing. If I weren't, I would regret not having made some contribution.'

'I don't like it.'

'You know it makes sense though, don't you?'

Of course, everything she said made sense. Except I didn't want her anywhere near danger.

PART FOUR

The Raid

10

October

It was one of those cool misty autumn evenings when we set out. Summer was over, but there was still a warmth in the air. The quiet streets of the town were lined with an array of trees of varying colours of leaves. Autumn would often pass unnoticed in the fast life of a big city, but not in a small coastal town like North Berwick. In this town the residents had time to take in the changing colours of the seasons and autumn was the one they appreciated most.

The car John had stolen was a seven-year-old Volvo with automatic transmission and tinted windows. It was a big car with a big engine, and he had filled the tank so we wouldn't have to stop at a garage. He had picked it up at the long-term car park at Glasgow airport. With the owners taking an international flight, it would likely be a week or more before it was reported stolen.

The key was exactly where he said it would be, on top of the offside rear wheel. I pulled away from the kerb and took the first right, stopping a few seconds later alongside the woman standing at the kerb. She was dressed in similar attire to myself, black hooded sweatshirt, black combat trousers and black trainers – Robertson always wore black.

After Emily put on her seatbelt, I said, 'Did you see where it was parked?'

'I saw.'

'Anything goes wrong and you have to drive, that's where you leave it. John will uplift and dispose of it before first light.' I looked at her face and the furrowed brow, and said 'I don't think he'll torch it, more likely he'll wipe it for prints and then leave it someplace it will be stolen within ten minutes.'

I looked across, the furrowed brow remained. The way she was sitting resembled a coiled spring.

We'd gone over everything – the video footage of the farmhouse, and the area we were going to park in. She would wait there until she got the call from me to drive to the front. She knew all the routes to get back to the A1. She was fully briefed, and knowing what to do should have helped, yet she appeared nervous.

When we pulled on to the A1 I looked over at her and said, 'You know, nights like this were perfect for the border reivers.'

She looked at me. 'Why?'

'Long nights, with mist and fog, they could carry out their raids with little chance of being seen ... or followed.'

'So the reivers were raiders?'

'Uh huh, they carried out countless cross-border raids from the late 1200s to the early 1600s. One of the most notorious Scottish reivers was the outlaw William Armstrong of Kinmont, aka Kinmont Willie. On a truce day in 1596 when safe conduct was given to anyone watching the criminal trials, Kinmont Willie was arrested and imprisoned in Carlisle Castle. The English authorities were so keen to get Willie that the arrest was in total violation of the truce. But Willie had some good friends in Scotland, one of whom being Walter Scott, the first—'

'Walter Scott, the writer?'

'No, Walter Scott, the first Lord Scott of Buccleuch. And this guy was not happy about his friend being illegally detained and held in England. If the SAS had been around four hundred odd years ago, big Walter would have been the man in charge. He was fearless and he lived for adventures, the more dangerous the better. On a night just like this he led a small group of hand-picked men on a raid on Carlisle Castle. Their goal: a prison break out - free Kinmont Willie and take him safely across the border back to Scotland. The walls of the castle proved too high for the reivers to scale, so Walter and his team broke through the castle wall, located Willie and took him home.

'The fact that no one had been killed during the raid proved to be of little consequence. At the time a fragile truce existed between England and Scotland and the breakout raid put that truce in jeopardy. So Walter, the man of honour that he was, took it upon himself to travel down to London and surrender to Queen Elizabeth. He was presented in front of her in court.

'The Queen was not in a good mood, and yelled at Walter - "How dare you break in to Carlisle castle and—"

'But Walter was not in a good mood either, he stepped forward and roared, "Tell me what it is that a man dare not do!"

'The court fell silent. Everyone was in shock with the suddenness of the exchange, and the realization that this Scotsman had just signed his own death warrant. The Queen, turned to her lord in waiting, and whispered, "Good God, with ten thousand such men I could conquer Europe."'

'What happened?'

'You have to understand how it was at that time. This was Elizabeth the First. She ruled with a rod of iron. Everyone sucked up to her, anyone who displeased her would likely be taken away to the Tower, tortured and beheaded. So no one did. For Walter, who was a big brute of a man, to stand up to her in the way that he had, threw her completely. She was probably bored with the grovelling that went on. Here was someone who had suddenly shattered the sheer monotony of her day. She liked that, and she liked Walter, for who he was, and for his loyalty to his friend.'

'She liked him ... she never married did she?'

'No.'

'Do you think they had an affair?'

'The Queen and Walter?'

'Yes.'

'We're talking about Elizabeth the First, the Virgin Queen, so I would say it would be unlikely, though if Hollywood got hold of it, then there is a possibility they might have had an affair; but if a certain Australian got hold of it they would *definitely* have had an affair. Who knows, she did allow him to return to Scotland though.'

I kept the conversation going, telling her all I knew about the man. When I ran out of stories about Walter I made some up. I'd already made him out to be a great big man, when I had absolutely no idea what he looked like. His adventures and acts of bravery were larger than life, I just assumed he was as well. Aside from being a distraction for Emily, it kept my own mind occupied. I was anxious; I'd never been on a mission like this before. It wasn't the fact that I didn't have my trusted rifle - or a firearm of any description - or that I was accompanied by a civilian - a woman - and not members of my squad. The main difference was that, other than the gangsters who'd threatened John's family, every mission had been either for Queen and country or for a secret government department, whereas tonight was personal. Before I'd always been detached, now I was emotionally involved.

Eventually, my imagination and stories about Walter dried up, but Emily kept the conversation going with a story about William Wallace. It was a lesser-known story, but I knew it nevertheless, so while my passenger recounted it I went through my checklist. Was I ready for this raid? Yes. I could pound the sand wall with my fists for almost two minutes. I had punching power and my timing and coordination were not far off being as good as they had ever been. I had tested all aspects in combat: Kane was still off work. I may be okay with my fists but more importantly how was I with my personal weapon? At two in the morning when the moon was full I had taken the three pounder out to a sand wall and tested her, going through a number of moves, hitting the wall where there was only sand, then moving on to the hard earth covered in long grass that lay at the top of the wall. My hands felt good, they easily absorbed the impact from the hard ground and the three pounder flew through the air without effort, hitting exactly what I aimed at. The months of working with the four pounder had paid off.

 I mentally went through the equipment, The car handled well. The spare tyre and tools had been checked. The petrol needle that had read full when we left North Berwick had barely moved. The three pounder lay in the boot, while we both carried new pay-as-you-go phones with each other's number programmed in. They would be destroyed afterwards, and the stone hammer would be thrown into a river. Afterwards ... I had to think that there would be an afterwards.

 About seven miles from Alnwick I took the slip road that John had pinpointed on the map. Following his well laid out directions I found the rough road that led to the back of the farmhouse. We parked under the group of trees that he had described perfectly. After that it was a quarter mile hike to the rear of the building. The window to a back workroom was closed but it slid open easily when I checked it. John was always thorough; I shouldn't have doubted him, yet everything had to be checked and rechecked. I went through all the rooms. Emily stood at the window in the living room, probably thinking of her daughter, and the man who had raped and killed Ailsa being in that room in less than an hour. We had made good time and arrived early, so I let her see the route to the farmhouse and the way in to it. But time was moving on and I worried that being so close to the past might become too much for her. I walked over and, standing at her shoulder said softly, 'It's time for you to go back to the car.'

She didn't move; her gaze still fixed out of the window, she said, 'I want to stay.'

'It's too dangerous for you to be here any longer.'

'What if you need help? What if three of them come at once. What if all of them come at once?'

'They won't. John is thorough. At the very most I'll have to handle two of them.'

'What if John got it wrong?'

'He never gets it wrong.'

'But what if this time he makes a mistake?'

'Then I'll do all of them.'

'All four?'

'Yes, all four.' Part of me knew it was a lie, but I wouldn't acknowledge it to myself and definitely not to Emily.

I walked back to the side of the door and laid the three pounder up against the wall. I looked back at Emily. She seemed to shrink into herself, a tiny figure standing beside the window, waiting for the monsters to arrive.

I called over to her, my voice no longer soft, 'Okay, Emily, you need to get going. Remember, I'll phone - two rings as soon as I see the first car approaching, then I'll switch off the phone. If you've not heard from me in 20 minutes—'

'No need to phone,' she said calmly. 'There are two cars arriving. Her voice faltered as she spoke again, the calm replaced by panic. 'There's two in each car. I knew this would happen. I knew it!'

I was by her side in a second. I grabbed her shoulders and spun her away from the window. Leaning down I looked directly into her eyes. 'You need to go right now, I can't fight with you here.' She was shaking her head wildly. 'Big Davey,' I held up my clenched fists, 'these were all I used on him. I wore a balaclava; there was no ambush, no tricks, no weapons. It was a fair fight, and it took me less than three seconds to finish him - and he was a fighter. Those four aren't, but I need you to go now. Get out of the bedroom window and don't look back until you're in the car.'

She looked deep in to my eyes, a look of forlorn hope, and ran into the hall. She'd be out of the window a second later. I turned, walked over to the doorway and picked up the hammer. I stood at the side of the door. I could hear their voices coming through the front door. Despite my display of confidence with Emily, I could feel my new found identities being stripped away. I was not the first lord of Buccleuch, nor was I Chaney. I had been, briefly, but Chaney would never have gotten himself in to this situation. Why? I asked myself the question yet I knew the answer. Chaney would not have allowed himself to fall in love. No, I wasn't Chaney, but it didn't matter. Not anymore. It didn't matter if I was half the man I used to be, I was still my father's son. Also, I was a man in love, and the four that were about to come through this door had raped and taken the life of her child. And for that all four were going to die right now, in agony ... in a river of blood.

I gripped the three pounder, it weighed nothing. I could feel the adrenaline flooding through my system.

I waited for the first man to come through the door. When he did, the hammer, possessing a life of its own, swung in an arc towards his forehead. I felt rather than saw the connection. I knew he'd gone down, but all my focus was now on the second man ... who had taken a few steps backwards. I moved towards him stepping over the body that lay between us. I swung the hammer downwards. As it neared its target two things happened. He moved to the side, and the other two men appeared behind him. I missed his head but the hammer impacted hard on his left shoulder. He staggered backwards. In a sweeping motion I brought the hammer upwards and sideways connecting with the side of his jaw. He went down. I stepped over him to get to the others – I was committed now. There was no way I could stop. I noticed a different look in the eyes of the third man. It was not fear, but rage, and he was going to be the most dangerous of all of them. He didn't look much like his photo in the newspaper, yet I recognized him immediately ... Cotton. Shifting his bodyweight he bent low and charged forwards like a bull. I swung down with the hammer but missed – he was too fast, ramming into my mid-section. I was winded; he drove forwards again, slamming me up against the wall. If I hadn't put in the work with the four pounder I'd have dropped the hammer, but I still had a good grip on it and it came down again, this time making contact near the middle of his back. He dropped down and I hit him again. I didn't see where the hammer hit as my head was suddenly thrown back. My world was spinning. I didn't know what had hit me, but I did know that if I didn't regain my senses Emily would be in danger. I forced myself to focus and made out through a fog of pain the fourth man swinging what looked like a bottle of whisky. I ducked as the bottle flew at the wall where my head had been, shattering as it did so. He followed through, his face against mine. Too close – he was right next to me, leaving me with no leverage. He pulled his head back and butted me. The impact stunned me, but only for a moment as he'd failed to put his bodyweight behind it. Instinctively, I tilted my right hand, lifting the hammer head upwards, relaxing my grip and letting the handle slide through my hand until I felt the cold steel head against my right index finger. I immediately swung with the hammer head and hit him in the temple area. There wasn't much force behind it, but there was enough. The blow stunned him, knocking him sideways. The fog had cleared now and, having already reversed the process with the hammer handle, I stepped to my right to attain maximum leverage and swung the hammer in a perfect arc hitting him in the ribs. I heard them break over his cry of pain, followed by the impact of him hitting the ground. Now there were the others. The nearest was the man I'd caught in the shoulder, he had just regained his feet. I went for his wounded side, and bending low swung the hammer in to the side of his left knee. As he went down I caught him in his ribs. This time the sound of his ribs cracking echoed through the farmhouse. No sound came from him, doubtless he was immersed in shock. As I looked around I realized that Cotton had disappeared. I found him in the kitchen, his back to me; a drawer open, knife in his left hand, trying to pull himself to a standing position. His right hand was folded over the edge of the worksurface for purchase as he hauled himself upwards. I moved fast, body and mind functioning as one, the timing of the swing in perfect unison with the amount of ground my legs were covering, the hammer slamming down hard on his right hand. He let out a high-pitched scream. Dropping the knife, he pulled both hands in to his chest. He was instinctively protecting his right hand but his right elbow was now exposed. The hammer made direct contact with the point of it. Another scream, this time more of despair than pain. He cried out 'Stop! Stop!'

'Stop?' I shouted. 'That's exactly what that poor eight-year-old girl asked you to do when you and your friends out there were stripping her. Stop, that's what she asked, and what happened, all of you laughed and tore her dress off her back followed by her underwear. What was it she cried? TELL ME!' I yelled as I brought the hammer down hard on his right ankle.

'Stop,' he whimpered. 'Please stop.'

Before there had been rage; now, less than a minute later, he was whimpering. Strange how quickly fear could change a man. I could hear it in his voice. I had heard it in my own in the abattoir in Andorra. Cotton was terrified ... with good reason.

'I'm sorry, I didn't catch that.' I said, as the hammer head crashed against his left ankle.

'PLEASE, PLEASE STOP!'

'Yea, that's what she cried, 'please stop', but did you? Did you stop, and let her get dressed and leave? No that's when you pushed her on to her stomach over the edge of a table, and then you did the unthinkable ... the unimaginable for a child. And all four of you laughed while you tore that child's innocence apart. She screamed then – she screamed for you to stop. Go on, scream!'

But I could no longer hear Cotton's screams. I was hearing Ailsa now, and I could feel the rage building in me. I wrenched Cotton on to his back and brought the hammer down full force on his left knee. He screamed with the pain that had shot up his spine and exploded in his brain. His voice full of despair, he began to repeat the word 'stop' so quietly it was almost a whisper. No, I was wrong. It wasn't a whisper. It was a prayer, he was praying now, but God wasn't going to save him. Nothing could save him now.

'And when you didn't stop, and your friends continued to laugh do you remember what she called out? Call that out now and I will stop.' I drew back the hammer.

He flinched and said it.

'Mum ... it's hurting me.'

'Yes, she said it quietly at first, but when her mother didn't appear, and hold her hand, and comfort her, and tell her this was all just a bad dream - when that didn't happen - she began to panic, and her cry became louder. Let me hear the way she called out then.'

'MUMMY! IT'S HURTING! IT'S HURTING!' He screamed as I brought the hammer down on his right shoulder.

'That's how she screamed - louder and louder until it became so loud you couldn't stand it anymore, so you ordered her to stop screaming, and when she wouldn't the beating began. With your fists at first, but when she continued to call out for her mother, you became enraged and picked up whatever was to hand and beat her head with it, and kept beating her ... until she lay still, and silent.'

I stood still and only then did I realize how heavily I was breathing. My heart pounded wildly in my chest. I felt sick to my stomach. I looked at Cotton, he was close to passing out with the pain. I had to finish him now, while he was conscious.

I stood above him and called out his name. He looked in to my eyes.

'All this - your three friends dead, and all this pain, and you about to die - has nothing to do with me. I'm just the messenger.' I laid the rectangular hammer head gently on his forehead for a couple of seconds before slowly swinging it back in an arc, holding it above my head, 'The message is from the girl's mother.' He stared at me. He may have been seconds away from passing out, yet I could see in his eyes he knew what was about to happen, and that was what mattered now. 'Here's her message', I said as summoning all my strength I swung the hammer straight down. I put everything behind it - all my bodyweight; all the rage and the fury that I'd kept in check since watching the video of Ailsa exploded into one swing of the hammer. I didn't look but heard the sound of his forehead splitting open ...

I don't know how long I stood over his body, still refusing to release my grip on the hammer that lay buried in the centre of his head. Perhaps as long as a minute, perhaps as little as three seconds. I stared at his lifeless body and said, 'If it had been up to me, I'd have taken you into an underground bunker and tortured you for a month before killing you.'

Distant sounds of someone in pain penetrated my consciousness. I wanted to be on the road back up. I wanted to be far away from this place, but the job wasn't over yet. If I left things as they were, it would be clear to the police that Cotton had been the target. I went over to the sink and rinsed the hammer head. I turned and my shoulders slumped on seeing Emily standing in the kitchen doorway. As hard as I tried to read her face, there was little to indicate how much she'd heard. As I walked towards her I looked in her eyes; the emptiness I saw there enough to tell me she'd heard too much. I brushed past her, gently laying my hand on her shoulder as I went.

Standing between the main room and the corridor I could see that the one that I'd hit first had been killed outright, the other two were crippled but still breathing. I used the hammer on them in the same way I used it on Cotton. It didn't take long. I moved quickly, emotionless, a man at work, like a joiner driving nails in to floorboards.

I stood still to catch my breath. My right shoulder felt odd, then I realized I had torn the deltoid, but it didn't matter. I looked around at the carnage. So much for the river of blood, there was hardly any.

One part of the raid was over. Now I had to get Emily back across the border and safely home.

*

I figured driving would take my mind off the pain, but there was so much adrenaline in my system that there was no pain – not physical anyway. There was something, though. It wasn't quite guilt, it was something far worse – shame. I had not needed to recount to Cotton what he'd done to Ailsa. Hearing it would have had a catastrophic effect on the woman sitting in the passenger seat. I had allowed her to come here so she could feel involved in the mission, become part of preventing these men from abusing other children. Instead, I had exposed her to the true horror of what had happened to her daughter. There was no way to undo what I'd done. Her sanity would be on a razor's edge – the next few hours would be crucial. And I had absolutely no idea what to say to her.

Shortly after crossing the border into Scotland she broke the silence. 'There's a lay-by coming up. Pull over'.

I did as she directed, then turned the engine off. We sat in silence. We had stopped in a layby on the A1 where the North Sea was clearly visible on our right. The sea was dark but relatively calm as the moon shone down on it, in direct contrast to the way I was thinking. If a patrol car passed they might stop to check if we had broken down. They may routinely run a registration check. I didn't know who the owner of the car was. The police asking the most innocent of questions could be enough to seal our future in prison. Yet I couldn't say anything.

Emily turned to look at me. 'I need to sort this out now, and I need to know where you stand.'

'Okay.'

'The mothers you spoke about, I couldn't hear them before, but I can hear them now. They're begging me to stop these men.'

'And we have, all four are dead. They're done abusing children. The mission was to eliminate Cotton and his friends. The mission's over, Emily. We completed it.'

'Did we? There's more just like Cotton. What about the other children and their mothers? It's those mothers I'm hearing now. Who's going to protect their children? And what about you? You've finished one mission; you now need another one. What is it you do with a broken soldier?'

Inwardly I breathed a sigh of relief. She was holding it together, thinking of the future. Creating targets, goals. As long as she had those she might manage to cope with the truth of what happened to her little girl. But as soon as she was caught those goals would disappear. Her idea had a chance of working right up to the point where she woke up in a prison cell.

A plan was even more important now. But a plan that when she was alone she would think through in detail, go over again and again checking for flaws. The plan was her steel shutter, and the horror of her daughter's death lay behind it. That shutter had to stand firm. If she saw a flaw then the reality of that future would fall away and her shutter with it, leaving her in the present – and the past – and with it the terrible unimaginable guilt that the one time her little girl had called for her help, she hadn't been there. I had no intention of letting that happen. The plan would be flawless.

I looked at her. 'You're right, I do need another mission – even if I didn't, whatever you decide to do, I am with you. But, if we're going exclusively after paedophiles, we're leaving a trail from the word go. Detectives will focus on the first group of murders and they'll investigate you until they find something. We need to throw them off track. We broaden the target. We hit sex traffickers, kill them in the same way with the stone hammer. We travel further; we hit the gangs in the big cities where sex trafficking is rife. We start with London. That'll put more suspicion on Robertson, and less on you. After that we hit paedophiles again, but we leave no trace. No bodies this time, just men disappearing.'

She nodded in agreement. 'No bodies, no murders to investigate. So where do we put the bodies?'

I turned my head to the right. Then turned to look back at her. I searched her black eyes to see what she was thinking. I couldn't get past the beauty of them, but it didn't matter this time. This time she knew exactly what I was thinking.

I turned the key in the ignition. The engine fired in to life and we were moving. The plan may appear flawless today, but eventually time would catch up with us. In the end we would both be sent to prison. But there were many missions to complete before then. It all depended on the shutter in her mind holding firm. If it fell away, she would fall with it.

John was due to pick this car up at 04:00. I would wait for him. Let him know the next move. All being well he would have a target for us inside a month. There had to be something happening. Emily had to stay busy, she had to see things moving forwards.

The road north stretched out before us, into the future; Emily had her plan, and she had her demons to deal with. I would stay the course with her – be that for a day or a year or decades. For now I was focused on getting her home, the headlights lighting only as far as the next bend in the road.

Author's Note

Reference is made in the story to an actual case where a convicted rapist was not given a custodial sentence but community service. The sentencing took place in the spring of 2023, shortly before publication. With the story set in 2020, licence was taken to include it due to its relevance.

About the Author

A H FitzSimons served in the British Army in the 1970s and 1980s before joining Lothian and Borders Police. He began writing in 2005 following a sixteen-month stay in hospital.

Also by A H FitzSimons

Fiction
The Game
Break Lima
HK9

Non-fiction
The Fight

www.ingramcontent.com/pod-product-compliance
Lightning Source LLC
Chambersburg PA
CBHW072102110526
44590CB00018B/3275